ALL THINGS LIONS FOR KIDS

FILLED WITH PLENTY OF FACTS, PHOTOS, AND FUN TO LEARN ALL ABOUT LIONS

ANIMAL READS

THIS BOOK BELONGS TO...

_____

_____

WWW.ANIMALREADS.COM

CONTENTS

Welcome To The World Of Lions!	1
What Is A Lion?	5
The Lions Of The World!	17
A Short History Lesson On The Evolution Of Lions	27
Where Do Lions Live?	39
What Do Lions Eat And How Do They Hunt?	43
Unique Characteristics Of Lions	49
The Life Cycle Of Lions	57
Thank You For Loving Lions So Much!	65
Thank You!	69

WELCOME TO THE WORLD OF LIONS!

A symbol of pride, power, and strength, the mighty lion is one of the most feared and respected members of the animal kingdom. You probably know them as the 'kings' of the jungle and the leaders of their pack, and although it is true that the lion has few predators in the wild (because who'd want to mess with *them*?!), it is also true that this is one amazing animal in need of protection.

The second-largest of all the cat species on earth, the lion is considered a **vulnerable** species. Which means their numbers are decreasing in their original homelands of Africa and India.

Lions are among the world's most incredible predators and are truly fascinating animals to get to know.

Want to discover all there is to know about the true **KING** of the jungle?

Then come on down and join us as we explore all there is to know about these fantastical creatures. We promise you'll have a **ROARing** good time becoming a lion expert!

**JUST
LION
AROUND!**

WHAT IS A LION?

A lion is a large cat from the **Felidae** animal family, which includes tigers, leopards, pumas, jaguars, cougars, and yes...even your everyday household cat! A native animal of India and Africa, the lion is known for its strong and muscular body (*they kind of look like they go to the gym regularly, don't they?!*), round heads and ears, an adorable tuff of fluff at the end of their tail and, in males, a spectacular hairdo called a **mane**.

Wondering how big and heavy a lion can get?

Well, let us tell you: **pretty BIG indeed!**

Lions can grow to about 3 ½ to 4 feet tall at their shoulders. Male lions, which are usually larger than females, can grow up to 10 feet in length with a two to three-feet long tail. Male lions can weigh anything between 330 and 550 pounds, while females usually weigh between 260 and 390 pounds. **That's some big cats alright!**

On average, a lion will grow as large as two standard-sized Christmas trees, although we certainly don't recommend you try to put one in your living room!

FUN FACT: The largest lion ever recorded was found in the wilds of South Africa way back in

1936. This very big fella weighed almost **SEVEN HUNDRED POUNDS!** That's about the weight of five full-grown adults.

Lions are very social animals and live in large packs called **prides**. They love to be around other lions (like you love to hang out with your friends!), but they don't only do it because being with friends is a lot of fun. For a lion, living in a pride means surviving is a lot easier: lions hunt in packs, since it's much easier to catch your lunch when there are many of you chasing prey.

Lions are excellent at working as a team, and in fact, they probably make the best hunting teams in the world.

Lions are what we call **apex predators**, which means that they have no natural predators in the wild. Although they hunt, they are not hunted by another animal – this is what apex means...**the very top animal in the natural food chain!**

Lions are also **carnivores** (*which means they eat meat*) and are **mammals**, which means that they do not lay eggs and feed their young with milk.

Hey, can you think of other kinds of mammals?

Well, if you said humans... you'd be absolutely right!

Humans like you and I are mammals. Other mammals in the world are bears, elephants, rodents, rhinoceros, dolphins, and many more!

A female lion is called a lioness, while a young lion is called a **cub.** The lioness may be slightly smaller than her male partner, but she is just as strong. More importantly, she plays a really important role in the pride. Without female lions, the male lions wouldn't survive at all!

All up, there are around 20,000 lions left in the wild today, which isn't very many at all. Researchers believe that this is only 5% of what the lion population *used* to be,

Most of them live in Africa, although there is a small number also living near a very special national park in India.

Don't worry... we'll find out all about that as we delve deeper into the wild lion world.

THE LION'S PRIDE (AND JOY)!

The pride is the lion's family, although it looks a little different from your own family in the case of this fascinating animal.

You see, lion prides are made up mostly of female lions and all their babies, alongside just a few males. The female lions have the task of raising their cubs together, which they do as one big friendly group. Lion cubs even drink milk from *any* other female lion in their pride when they're hungry, not only their mothers. Isn't that super cool?

Meanwhile, males have one task only: **to protect their pride at all costs!** Males usually stay with the pride into which they are born for about three or four years. After that, they leave and try to find an adult pride of their own, where they can have cubs with adult females and then stick around to protect their new pride.

Most lion prides have about 20 members, although some of the largest ones can have up to 40. Since they love to live in such big groups, lions are considered the single most sociable big cat in the world.

Lion prides work so well together that they often **roar together** too – *pride roars are absolutely astonishing to hear*! Lions roar to mark territory and can usually be heard from a distance of several miles. And it's not just adults that do the roaring...cubs join in on the fun too!

Can you imagine 40 cats all meowing all at the same time? That would be a pretty intense sound!

HOW MANY SPECIES OF LIONS ARE THERE IN THE WORLD?

Now, this might surprise you: **there is only one species of lion in the world!** The scientific name for this animal is Panthera Leo, and within this species, there are two quite distinct sub-species: the *African* lion and the *Asiatic* lion. As you may easily guess, one lives in Africa and the other in Asia!

What is very interesting is that although there is only one major species of lion, there are several different breeds that have evolved slightly different characteristics. In this case, they are not unlike domestic cats: sure, they are all the same species, BUT there can be very many different breeds. **Some can even look wildly unique!**

And so it is with lions, although all breeds do look very alike indeed.

Let's meet a few, shall we?

WHAT DOES THE LION CALL THE BARBER?

His **MANE** man!

THE LIONS OF THE WORLD!

We learned earlier that there is only one species of lion but many different breeds, right? Well, it's now time to check out some of the most unique kitties out there!

We will explore 5 different breeds of lions, and although they can look very similar to one another, they have slight differences as they "grew up" in separate regions and conditions.

Are you ready to dive in and learn all about these furry cats?

Let's explore them one by one!

THE AFRICAN LION

The African Lion lives in central and southern Africa and is the second-largest lion breed in the world. Of all the lion breeds, the African is one of the most endangered and suffers greatly from loss of habitat (*when its forests are cut down*), and hunting (*humans kill them for their fur and bones*).

THE KATANGA LION

This lion breed lives exclusively in the southwestern region of the African continent, so it's found in countries like Angola, Namibia, Zambia, and western Zimbabwe (maybe you can ask an adult to show you where these countries are on a map?) This is one of the largest lion breeds of all.

THE WHITE LION

The sparkling white fur is the first characteristic that gives this breed away! This is a very rare breed of lions that has something scientists call a **recessive gene** – which means the whiteness is in their DNA and only *sometimes* comes out. White Lions are known to live in only two protected reserves in South Africa, and there are organizations that purposely drive around the parks looking for them for the sole reason of protecting them. White Lions do not fare well in the wild because their color makes them stand out too much, so they find it difficult to hunt for food. Today, although there are hundreds of white lions in zoos and sanctuaries around the world, scientists believe only about two dozen are left living in the wild.

THE MASAI LION

The Masai Lion is a slightly different breed of lion that lives in eastern Africa. They are not as bulky as the African lions, and they have slightly longer legs, so they look slender in comparison.

THE ABYSSINIAN LION

This is one of the most fascinating lion breeds of all because they have only been 'discovered' recently. How can that be, you ask? Well, what usually happens is that animals that seem to be of the same breed are sometimes tested by scientists. Then when slight differences are found in the DNA (*the building blocks of our bodies!*), experts realize they are dealing with different breeds altogether.

This is exactly what happened in 2012 when researchers took samples from many lions in one particular area of Africa: **they discovered a breed they didn't know existed!** The Abyssinian is a very rare breed of lion, and only a handful exist in a lion sanctuary in Addis Ababa, which is the capital of Ethiopia. Researchers aren't really sure how these lions came to be so different, but they are trying to find out, right now!

THE ASIATIC LION

Finally, one lion breed that doesn't live in Africa!

Oh, but wouldn't you know it... it actually does 😉

The Asiatic is the rarest lion breed in the world. Most live in the beautiful and very protected Giri Forest in India, although a few also live in private reserves in Africa! Smaller than all their African cousins, Asiatic lions only weigh about 250 pounds, which still makes them quite large kitties indeed. Given they are small(er) and even more agile than usual, the Asiatic lion is one of the fastest breeds in their family. Currently, experts believe there are only 600 Asiatic lions left in the Indian wilderness.

FUN FACT: Although lions do not like to climb trees often, they can do so relatively easily. Why on earth would a lion ever want to climb a tree? To get away from biting insects on the ground and have a higher lookout over the savanna!

WHAT TIME IS IT WHEN A LION WALKS INTO THE ROOM?

Time to get out of the room!

A SHORT HISTORY LESSON ON THE EVOLUTION OF LIONS

By now, you know that there is only one lion species in the world, but, like us, you're probably wondering if there were more species in the past.

Was there ever a prehistoric lion? If yes, what did it look like?!

As it turns out, lions were once one of the most widespread mammals in the world. Scientists have found evidence that lions were *everywhere* in the Pleistocene period. This was about 2.5 million to 12,000 years ago!

The population of the lions was spread throughout Africa, America, and Eurasia, which was the landmass that separated and has now become two continents: Asia and Europe. Scientists found that there were two Pleistocene cave lions and another 12 species from the Middle East and Africa. Unfortunately, they all went **extinct** (which meant they all died out) at one point or another.

Interestingly, scientists also found there were six modern lion species in India and Africa, and they believe these were the ancestors of our world's modern-day lions.

Wouldn't it be awesome if all lion species survived to this day? It sure would be! That's why it's really important that we protect the lions we have left on our planet (and all the other creatures as well!)

WHAT DID PREHISTORIC LIONS LOOK LIKE?

Lions roamed the planet during the last Ice Age, and even back then, they were one of the largest predators. This just makes lions way more awesome, right? I guess it's really true that they are indeed the king of the beasts: **past and present!**

North America was once also home to lions, who roamed the lands from Alaska in the north, all the way to Mexico in the south. Scientists found evidence that prehistoric lions used to hunt bison and wild horses, so we know they must've been tough as nails.

Evidence has also taught us those prehistoric lions had round ears and faded stripes, much like those we see in tigers today. They had tufted tails, and male lions already had their distinct fluffy manes. If you look them up, prehistoric lions looked more like the modern-day jaguars or leopards or even Diego the saber tooth from the movie Ice Age!

One thing you will notice is that prehistoric lions looked a lot more slender than modern-day lions, which means they were probably built for speed more than anything else.

Lions have indeed evolved over time, but not so much that they are completely unrecognizable from their modern-day cousins.

WHAT OTHER ANIMALS ARE CLOSELY RELATED TO LIONS?

Yes, we all know that lions are one of the many big cats that roam our planet today. They are even cousins of our pet cats. But which are their *closest* relatives? And are there any surprising ones?

The lions' closest living relative is none other than the jaguar, followed by the tiger and the leopard. These big cats are all descendants of the same prehistoric lions we've learned about.

FUN FACT: Did you know that big cats like pumas and cheetahs can't roar, but they actually purr? Much like your cat! On the contrary, the bigger cats in the family, such as the lion and the tiger, can only roar and not purr. Pretty cute, huh?

FEMALE & MALE LIONS: TOGETHER, THEY MAKE IT WORK!

A female lion is called a lioness, and did you know that no matter how tough male lions are, they rely on the lioness within their pride for a lot of things? They need each other to survive, as is the case with most animals living on our planet.

Lionesses are considered the gatekeepers of the pride. They have very strong maternal instincts, and at the same time, they don't usually just let outsiders in the pride easily, especially other lionesses. See, within a pride, oftentimes, membership only changes when birth or death occurs.

And lastly, lionesses are known to be very good hunters, even better than the pride leader. **Woah!** Such a surprise, right? So, male lions do rely on lionesses **A WHOLE LOT!**

That being said, the main role of lionesses within a pride is to hunt for food for the male lions and their cubs. They are also responsible for raising their cubs. Remember, only the cubs of the male lions within the pride are welcome in the pride.

What makes a lioness better suited for hunting is that they are usually 30% faster than male lions, and this is why they evolved to be a little bit smaller than male lions. Lionesses are very caring and protective mamas, and they keep the pride together.

But surely the males also have plenty of important stuff to do in a pride, right? And yes, they sure do!

Male lions are effective at protecting or defending their territory. They are bigger and better suited for a fight than females, and they take their 'bodyguard' duties very seriously.

This is their main responsibility, and they're awesome at it!

Even though lionesses are the pride's primary hunters, male lions also hunt from time to time. But unlike lionesses that go in groups, lions hunt for their meal individually.

HOW DO YOU BRUSH A LION'S TEETH?

VERRRY carefully!

WHERE DO LIONS LIVE?

It's funny to know that lions are known as the 'kings of the jungle' although lions don't actually live in them!

In Africa, lions live in grasslands and huge wide-open plains of the savanna. Lions prefer grasslands, open forests, and scrubs over other habitats because these environments provide them with easy access to their favorite prey. Since lions are among the fastest predators in the savanna, they don't rely on 'hiding' to catch prey. In fact, they prefer wide open spaces where they can freely chase smaller animals who, in turn, have nowhere to hide.

PS. We'll chat about what lions eat in the next section, but boy, do they need to eat a *lot* to support their large bodies!

Scrubs provide lions with areas of desert patches that are ideal for them to hunt in, but at the same time, they'll have enough cover that serves as their shelter.

Lions do love hunting but what they love most is socializing. As a matter of fact, lions are very social animals, and they love to lie about playing with their young and nurturing them.

We would certainly hope that we'll see more and more lions in the wild soon. And maybe have a few populations outside India and Africa. For that, all of us have got to do our part to make the world a better place to live in for lions and all creatures alike.

ON WHICH DAY DO LIONS EAT THE MOST?

Chews-day!

WHAT DO LIONS EAT AND HOW DO THEY HUNT?

Lions mostly hunt and eat animals that have hooves. The habitats that we discussed above have a good population of their prey. They often hunt wildebeests, zebras, and antelopes. These animals, as fast as they may run, are often easy targets for a group of lionesses on the prowl.

That's how tough these mama lions are, and they seldom miss their catch.

Just how tough hunters are lions, anyway? Well, just take into consideration the fact that they even hunt large animals such as giraffes and rhinoceroses. Buffalos in the open forests and woodlands also won't stand a chance if lions set their eyes on them.

Remember, these are no easy targets to take down, but with a group of determined (and hungry!) lionesses, nothing is impossible. Lions work together with amazing precision, forming a semi-circle around the prey, so it has little chance of escape. When chasing prey, a lion will usually not bite first but, rather, trip the running prey, so it stumbles. Only once the prey has been 'tripped' will a lion grab its prey with its powerful claws or teeth,

Witnessing a lion hunt is one of the most amazing natural spectacles in the world. It can sometimes be hard to watch a lion hunt a sweet little animal like a zebra, but when you remember that this is nature at work, you will feel that it is exactly as nature intended.

When you grow up, perhaps you will one day visit Africa and enjoy an unforgettable safari!

Lions typically hunt every two to three days but know that they can go without eating for a week or even a month if there's no food available at all.

This is given that they have access to water constantly.

Although they mostly hunt at night, lions also sometimes like hunting during storms. True story! Experts believe that stormy weather can make hunts much easier, because prey find it more difficult to spot predators during heavy rains. How smart is that?!

Lions can easily hide in the tall yellow grass!

As far as their appetite goes, lions will eat as long as there is meat. They have voracious appetites and will hunt whenever food is available. Lions are very stealthy hunters, and their prey wouldn't even know what hit them!

FUN FACT: Lions can eat about a quarter of their weight or about 88 pounds of meat in one meal. They do need to eat a lot to convert the calories to energy for their next hunt. After all, they don't eat at regular intervals like you, and I do. So, when they eat, they sure eat a lot!

WHAT DO LIONS WEAR TO SLEEP?

PAW-jamas!

UNIQUE CHARACTERISTICS OF LIONS

Let's take a closer look at the mighty body of the king of the beasts!

As we already know, it takes a lot of might and muscles for a lion to be able to guard its territory and its pride. This applies to both male and female lions. While male lions have larger and more powerful and muscular bodies, lionesses have bodies that enable them to hunt better. They are a lot lighter and more agile than their male counterparts.

Lions have what you call a compact body with powerful forelegs that they need to thrust themselves onto their prey and powerful teeth and claws that will help them catch their prey and eventually devour them.

Scary, huh? **Roar!**

Their beautiful coats are usually yellow-gold in color, with some having blonde to reddish-brown, or even black in rare lion breeds. Did you know that young lions will naturally have some light spots on their coats that disappear as they grow older? Yes, they do! But they are so light that sometimes you may not even notice the spots unless you take a good close look at them, which, let's be honest, would not be an easy or very safe thing to do!

A lion's gorgeous mane is determined by many things, including age and location. For some reason, the more north a lion lives in Africa, the bigger the mane. Mane size and fullness is also determined by age and genes, which are the biological traits all animals get from their parents. So, just like your hair was passed on to you by your mom and dad, a lion may also pass on the length and fullness of their manes to their young.

The most significant symbol of a male lion is indeed its mane. A lion's mane actually serves many functions for their bodies and day-to-day activities. Naturally, their manes grow more magnificent as they grow older. The color gets darker, and it attracts more and more females to them for possible partners. A lion's mane is also meant to protect their heads from injuries when they fight!

Without the beautiful coats of lions, no one except expert scientists can tell apart a lion from a tiger. They are actually *that* similar.

Can you see the similarities between tigers and lions?

HOW DO LIONS KEEP THEIR BODIES STRONG?

While lions do a lot of lying around, they are not lazy at all. They are just really smart at conserving their energy in case they need to hunt or protect their pride. Hunting takes a *lot* of energy and effort, and as good as the lions are when it comes to catching their prey, sometimes, they are not successful in 100% of their attempts.

What lions do is rest whenever they can so they can hunt again when the opportunity comes.

Lions actually have very few sweat glands, and this helps them conserve a lot of their strength so they can become active and hunt during nighttime, where it will take less energy to catch their prey when it's not blistering hot. They also have amazing eyes that work well in the dark to help them as they catch their next meal.

One could say that lions are physically gifted, and with their strong jaws and teeth, they can easily catch and make a meal out of their prey. What really helps is that they are carnivorous; they eat meat which gives them a lot of energy to grow big and strong.

FUN FACT: Lions can go without eating anything for a whole month and still survive. However, they can't go very long without water. But what if there isn't any water around like, say, in times of drought? Well, lions are not just going to sit around and wait for rain! These incredible animals can actually extract water from plants. Their favorite is the tsamma melon. That's how smart and resourceful lions are!

YOU RULE!

THE LIFE CYCLE OF LIONS

Just like you, lions start out small and grow big and strong as time passes.

Now let's see how much lions differ from us humans, shall we?

Much like cats, baby lions are born with their eyes closed. They usually open about two to three weeks after birth. Mama lions are VERY protective at this early stage, as you may have experienced if you've ever lived with a cat who has given birth to kittens. Usually, domestic mama cats will trust their humans (*but no one else!*) whereas, in the wild, **lion mamas don't trust anyone or anything at all!**

Mama lions take care of their cubs for up to two years, so it's safe to say that this is the age where lions are still considered kids like you.

In about three to four years, lions will be fully developed and considered adults. At this age, they can mate and make babies of their own. This is where the life of a lion gets tricky, if not challenging. You see, the paths of male and female lions are quite different when they become adults.

Male lions must leave the pride when they turn three years old *or* challenge the current leader for their position. If a male lion chooses to leave the pride, they either live alone or find another pride leader to challenge. Although lions are social creatures, there have been instances where lions have preferred to live alone!

On the other hand, Lionesses can stay within the pride and fulfill their role as a hunter and nurturer in the group. There are lionesses, though, who also choose to leave the pride to either live alone or join others.

Once again, this is where it gets really hard for wild lions. No matter what, between hunting and fighting for territory, a lion's life in the wild is not easy. This is reflected in the lifespan of a lion in the wild which only averages 10 years. Lions in captivity, if they are well taken care of, may live for up to 25 years old.

Unfortunately, fights lead to injuries, and many times this leads to early death for many lions. In the wild, however, this is the circle of life and survival of the fittest!

FUN FACT: Lions are the second-largest cat in the world. Only the Siberian tiger is bigger!

WHAT THREATS DO LIONS FACE?

Lion numbers have been decreasing over the last few years in Africa. Experts believe that numbers have halved in just three short generations. The main threat to wild lion populations is poaching by humans. This happens because man and lion sometimes share land in Africa, and in order to protect farm animals and people, locals will hunt and kill local resident lions before they have a chance to attack.

Unfortunately, people have been moving into lion territory quite a lot, which means humans and lions sometimes must compete for land and, in turn, for food too. Although a lion would surely win a combat face to face, humans have developed firearms like guns and rifles, which means they can easily kill lions without running any risks.

The second biggest threat for lions is climate change, especially in relation to droughts and late rainy seasons. When droughts go on for too long, grazing animals tend to migrate further away, which means lions must travel a lot further to find their next meal.

Unfortunately (and this is perhaps the saddest part), lions are also illegally hunted for their fur and bone, which is very heart-breaking. There are some cultures that believe lion body parts make good medicine, so even though killing lions in the wild is illegal, they still do it! This is called poaching and, in Africa, this is a very big problem.

Luckily, there are many organizations that fight poaching and help protect the mighty lion and other animals in the wild.

WHY DID THE LIONESS CROSS THE ROAD?

She was at the ZEBRA crossing!

THANK YOU FOR LOVING LIONS SO MUCH!

Did you enjoy your journey with the pride? There sure are a lot of cat species in this world, but there's nothing like the mighty lions. What fascinated you about them the most? Is it their powerful roar? Their hunting skills? Or their intimidating appearance?

We enjoyed *everything* we learned about lions, and we hope that you did, too! So, thank you so much for taking the time to get to know them with us! Don't forget to share your knowledge about lions with your friends and family. We bet they too, will love to find out all there is to know about the King of the ~~jungle~~ savanna!

HOW YOU CAN HELP PROTECT LIONS IN THE WILD

If you love lions as much as we do, you'll probably want to know if there is anything you can do to help protect them in the wild. In fact, there is!

You can start planning a once-in-a-lifetime trip to Africa to see lions living in the wild. When you **visit a protected nature reserve in Africa, you must buy an entry ticket, and this is GREAT news because visitor fees are put back into the reserve and help protect all the animals living within their fence, lions included.

**There are several organizations and charities that work directly with animal welfare groups in

Africa. Some of these charities offer lion 'adoptions,' which is a super fun gift to ask for Christmas or your next birthday. All the money raised goes towards educating local Africans, so they can learn the importance of *not* hunting lions and buying more wilderness so lions can roam free of danger. Some of the best lion charities you and your family can look up are:

- African Parks
- Wildlife Conservation Network
- Lion Guardians
- African Wildlife Foundation

HAVE A
ROAR-SOME
DAY!

THANK YOU!

Thank you for reading this book and for allowing us to share our love for lions with you!

If you've enjoyed this book, please let us know by leaving a rating and a brief review wherever you made your purchase! This helps us spread the word to other readers!

Thank you for your time, and have an awesome day!

For more information, please visit:

www.animalreads.com

HOW DOES A LIONESS GREET THE ANTELOPE IT MEETS ON THE SAVANNAH?

"Pleased to eat you!"

© Copyright 2022 - All rights reserved Admore Publishing

ISBN: 978-3-96772-095-2

ISBN: 978-3-96772-096-9

Animal Reads at www.animalreads.com

The content contained within this book may not be reproduced, duplicated or transmitted without direct written permission from the author or the publisher.

Under no circumstances will any blame or legal responsibility be held against the publisher, or author, for any damages, reparation, or monetary loss due to the information contained within this book. Either directly or indirectly.

Published by Admore Publishing: Roßbachstraße, Berlin, Germany

www.admorepublishing.com

www.ingramcontent.com/pod-product-compliance
Lightning Source LLC
LaVergne TN
LVHW020142080526
838202LV00048B/3991